THE NON-ELECTRIC LIGHTING SERIES

BOOK 2:
Olive Oil Lamps &c.

Text & Photos by Ron Brown
Cover by FK
Copyright © 2014 Ronald B. Brown
All rights reserved.
ISBN 978-0-9853337-7-5

R&C Publishing
Newark Valley, New York

Notice: This manual is designed to provide information on vegetable-oil lamps and fat lamps (i.e. lamps that burn semisolid fats such as butter, lard, margarine, etc.)

It is not the purpose of this guide to reprint all the information that is otherwise available, but to complement, amplify, and supplement other texts and resources. You are urged to read all the available material and learn as much as you can about vegetable-oil lamps and to tailor the information to your specific circumstances.

Every effort has been made to make this guide as complete and accurate as possible. However, there may be mistakes, both typographical and in content. Therefore this text should be used only as a general guide and not as the ultimate source of vegetable-oil lamp and fat lamp information. Furthermore, this guide contains information that is current only up to the printing date.

The purpose of this manual is to educate and entertain. The views, opinions, positions, of strategies expressed by the author are his alone. The author makes no representations as to the accuracy, completeness, correctness, suitability, or validity of any information in this book and will not be liable for any errors, omissions, or delays in this information or any losses, injuries, or damages arising from its use.

ISBN 978-0-9853337-7-5

Published by R&C Publishing
15 Dr. Knapp Road South
Newark Valley, NY 13811

Printed in the United States of America

Table of Contents

So Let's Get Started...9
Design #1 – Cotton Puff 9
Design #2 – Pyrex Measuring Cup 12
Design #3 – Beer-Bottle Lamp 13
Bad Info – Corn Oil 15
Design #4 – Tuna Can &c. 16
Design #5 – Floating (Cork) 19
Design #6 – Floating (Ancient Pattern) 21
Design #7 – Floating (Kearny) 22
Bad Info – Water Candle (DANGEROUS)........23
Design #8 – String Lamps 28
Fiberglass Wicks...32
Design #9 – Orange Peel 32
Bad Info – Veggie Oil in Kero Lamps.................33
Fat lamps..34
Design #10 – Tuna Can Fat Lamp 34
Design #11 – Tuna Can Fat Lamp Variation.......35
Design #12 – Butter Candle.................................37
Design #13 – Philippine Design 39
Design #14 – I-Didn't-Know-Olive-Oil-Burned 41
Design #15 – Copper End-Cap Fat Lamp............45
A Word About Fuels..49
Closing Notes..51
Afterword...52

Table of Contents

Foreword

Years ago, while still in college, I helped a friend move to a new apartment. Just about the time the last box was hauled up the stairs, the power went out. Fortunately for us, it was not yet dark outside but still, it was spooky as heck for this 20 year old.

Thinking this was one grand adventure, we settled in to wait it out. My friend's apartment had a gas stove so with a little ingenuity, we opened a can of tomato soup and fried up some melted cheese sandwiches for dinner. Then it got dark.

I decided to stick around for moral support and also, because my own place would likely be dark and spooky too. What did we know? We were kids.

Back in those days, we all had transistor radios so we listened to music and gossiped while waiting for some news about the sudden blackout. The thought of the world ending or a massive EMP did not even cross our minds and ultimately, we learned that a motorist had run into a telephone pole and taken out a substation.

I do not believe the term "Prepping" had been invented yet. For college kids of the era, being prepared meant having the aforementioned radio, a bottle of Annie Green Springs and a good sense of humor.

That being said, all of the strange noises in a strange place were unsettling so we ventured outdoors to retrieve an old flashlight from the glove compartment of my car. It was pretty well run down so we decided not to use it except for true necessities – such as finding our way down the hall to the bathroom without running into a wall.

So there we were: two girls, sitting shoulder to shoulder on the couch in the dark, quietly talking, each determined not to let the other one know she was frightened at being isolated in a totally new place and in complete darkness.

How much comfort there would have been in a simple candle-sized flame! During the entire time we huddled there, it never occurred to us that we actually had a good source of light, one that would have scared away the boogie man we thought for sure was lurking right outside the door. It was right there all along. And so simple as I now know. But *then* I had no idea.

In one of the yet-unpacked boxes, my friend had a tub of vegetable shortening and a bottle of olive oil – both perfectly good lamp fuels. It would have been so easy to make a small lamp – so ridiculously easy. But we didn't know that. We were two liberated, educated, and sophisticated college girls. We were also clueless. I look back and laugh and shake my head in disbelief.

My point is this. The book *Olive Oil Lamps &c.* will only take half an hour to read. And yet when the lights go out (and trust me they will at one time or another), it might turn out to be one of the best thirty-minute investments you ever make.

Blackouts don't always happen when you're home snuggled up next to your stockpile of candles and Coleman lanterns. Knowing how to create some light from ordinary pantry ingredients just might save the day as well as a few scary moments.

Oh – one more thing. Oil lamps are fun to make, budget friendly, and pretty to look at too! I love this little book and know that you will too.

Gaye Levy
May 2014

꙳꙳꙳

Want to learn more about basic preparedness? Please visit Gaye's website at www.backdoorsurvival.com where you will find tools for creating a self-reliant lifestyle through thoughtful prepping and optimism.

"Let there be light . . ." (Genesis 1:3)

So Let's Get Started

The first part of this book deals with olive oil lamps. But "olive oil lamps" will actually burn all sorts of vegetable oil, not just olive oil. That's why &c. is part of the book title.

Later on, we'll discuss fat lamps. Fat lamps can burn semisolid fats (butter, lard, Crisco) in addition to vegetable oil. That's another reason &c. is part of the title.

So what does &c. stand for? It's an alternate abbreviation for etcetera. Some would say archaic rather than alternate. Archaic. Old. Like me.

Vegetable oil lamps date from Biblical times. For lamp purposes, buy the cheapest cooking oil available. You're not going to eat it; you're going to burn it.

Vegetable oil lamps are less expensive than candles to operate. One tablespoon of vegetable oil will produce a candle-sized flame for two hours. That's less than a penny per hour.

Design #1 – Cotton Puff

Pour ¼-inch of cooking oil in the bottom of a cereal bowl. A clear glass bowl is best – where light can escape through the sides of the bowl – but an opaque ceramic bowl or even an empty tuna fish can will suffice.

Soak up a cotton ball or puff (the kind with which m'lady removes her makeup) in the oil. Roll it around in the oil and make sure it is saturated. When I demonstrated this lamp to my sister she said, "Don't you need a wick or something?" Yes, you do. The cotton puff is the wick.

Surprisingly, a ball of paper towel (from a 2" x 2" square of toweling), rolled up between your palms like a child rolls up a ball of clay, also works. A puff made of synthetic fibers, however, will not work. Synthetic fibers (e.g. polyester) melt in the heat of the flame. The melting seals off the capillary action by which fuel is drawn to the flame.

One lady complained to me that her lamp simply would not work. "What did you use for the cotton?" I asked. "For the cotton puff?"

"The packing that came in the top of my vitamin bottle," she responded.

Good grief. Methinks I've identified the problem.

After the COTTON puff is saturated with oil, pinch a small nipple or point on it and light the point with a match. (The base of the puff sets in the oil and the point or nipple is on top.)

Here you will encounter Problem #1. Vegetable oil is fiendishly difficult to ignite. This is not all bad. It makes a vegetable-oil lamp a very safe lamp. If you knock it over, it will make a mess but it won't start a fire. In your first attempt at lighting a vegetable-oil lamp, you will soon find yourself surrounded by an array of oil-soaked matches and oil-soaked matchboxes.

SOLUTION: Put a drop or two of a flammable or combustible liquid on the nipple, then light it with a match. The liquid flares up for a couple of seconds and burns itself off, leaving behind a small candle-sized flame from the now-burning vegetable oil.

"Flammable" includes gasoline, nail polish remover, dry gas, and cigarette lighter fluid. "Combustible" includes charcoal lighter fluid, kerosene, and diesel fuel. Whatever works.

Be cool. There are 76 drops in a teaspoon. One drop of gasoline is not going to explode and blow the windows out of your house.

How do you get one drop? With an eyedropper. Or with a tiny bit on the end of a teaspoon, dripped onto the puff.

Problem #2. After thirty minutes of burning, the vegetable oil begins to warm and volatilize more easily. The flame spreads, gets bigger, and begins to smoke.

SOLUTION: Put a metal collar around the flame. A ¼-inch washer from the workshop is ideal. Pull the oil-soaked cotton nipple through the hole in the center of the washer before lighting it.

You can also fashion a metal collar from a piece of aluminum foil, the size of a postage stamp. Poke a hole through the center with a pencil point. The objective is to prevent the flame on the puff from getting too big.

This lamp will provide light for many hours. It's cheap, simple, easy to make.

Its disadvantage lies in the struggle encountered when adjusting the size of the flame – pulling more cotton through the washer to get a larger flame or pushing some cotton back through the hole if you pulled too much out. The washer gets hot. The oil is messy. But despite any drawbacks, it does work.

Design #2 – Pyrex Measuring Cup

Pour ¼-inch of vegetable oil into a Pyrex measuring cup, wad up a 2" x 2" square of paper toweling, light the paper, and drop the burning clump on top of the oil. Done.

Advantages: It's super-fast and it works. You can take it outside in a breeze and it remains lit.

Disadvantages: There is no control over the flame size. Because of that, the lamp smokes, limiting it to outside use. And the glass itself will gradually become smoked up.

The lamp, including its bottom and its handle, becomes very hot. You will need a trivet under it and gloves to carry it. But it will get you to the privy and back at midnight.

■ **ABOVE:** *Virtually any paper can be used as a wick (bond paper, paper bag, writing tablet) but the glass must be Pyrex (a measuring cup or coffee pot). A clear glass coffee cup or beer mug or creamer (from a sugar and creamer set) will break.* ■

Design #3 – Beer-Bottle Lamp

Fill an empty beer bottle (the twist-off-cap type) with vegetable oil. It is important that the inside of the bottle be DRY. Fill the bottle to the brim. Don't leave any head space.

Poke a hole through the bottle cap with a nail or scratch awl. Insert a wick into the hole, then screw the cap onto the bottle and light the wick. Use a drop or two of flammable liquid to facilitate lighting.

The inside of the bottle cap is apt to contain a gummy substance used to seal the bottle. For lamp use, scrape out the gummy material as best you can.

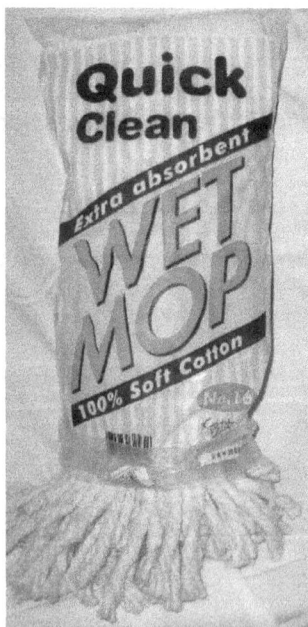

■ **ABOVE:** *For a wick, the best I've found is a strand from a cotton-string floor mop. String mop-heads can be purchased at the Dollar Store. For a buck you'll have a lifetime supply of wicks. The coarse weave of the mop head is ideal for the heavy, viscous vegetable oil. The closer, denser weave of conventional kerosene lamp wicks doesn't work very well for vegetable oil. ■*

A tightly-rolled strip of cotton (not polyester) from your handkerchief will also work. Ditto for a strip of your flannel pajamas or flannel shirt or denim from your jeans. Just nothing synthetic.

Did I say nothing synthetic? A small round fiberglass wick can be used although it's difficult to thread through the hole in the bottle cap. It will likely get mashed up and need trimming. And getting a square-across cut with scissors is g-r-r difficult. And it's finicky – hard to pull more out if the flame is too small or tamp back in if the flame is too big. With cotton you can just snip off the end and start over if things go badly.

A cotton wick will lift vegetable oil vertically 2½" or less. So, although a beer bottle looks very candle-like, with its small diameter neck it will only burn a couple of hours.

Bad Info – Corn Oil

"We have burned the following oils [in lamps]: sunflower, canola, safflower, peanut, sesame, walnut, grape seed, corn, hemp & soy . . . Corn oil is the worst in our experience." – *I Didn't Know Olive Oil Would Burn*, Merry Bickers, 2008

"By the way, for those who are quite serious about non-petroleum fuel. It is true that you can burn many vegetable oils. [but] CORN oil absolutely does not work." – http://i.treehugger.com/files/2006/06/petroleumfree_1_1.php

That didn't sound quite right to me. So I tried corn oil in a beer bottle lamp where the wick would have to lift the oil and I could measure how far it was lifted. I used a cotton mop strand as a wick. And it lifted the corn oil just as far and burned just as long as anything else.

So why the bad rap? Lighting. Or so I believe. I found corn oil maddeningly difficult to light. Using a drop or two of denatured alcohol on every attempt, it took eight big wooden kitchen matches to get the beer-bottle lamp started. But we need to distinguish between "absolutely does not work" and "difficult to light." They are two different things.

Design #4 – Tuna Can &c.

■ **ABOVE:** *Dave Hax, a UK-based survivalist, presents five "emergency candle" designs on YouTube. Two were covered in* Book 1: Candles. *His third design is to poke a hole in the top of a can of oil-packed tuna, insert a string for a wick, and light it. I used a 50-ply candle wick in preference to a "string" but, even at that, the flame was tiny.* ■

■ **ABOVE:** *The little flame needn't surprise us. As discussed above (Design #3), we need a heavy-and-fluffy wick for vegetable oil. Indeed, as we see here, a cotton strand from a string-type floor mop solves the small-flame problem very nicely. Note that the wick siphons oil in excess of what is consumed by the flame. The amount of excess shown here is after ten minutes of operation. Were this lamp to run a couple of hours, oil would be streaming down the side of the can and onto the table.* ■

■ **ABOVE:** *But in fact, the lamp sputtered and went out after only one hour. The sputtering was due to water being present in the oil. But was all the fuel consumed? I opened the tuna can so I could drain and measure the remaining liquid. I found that, theoretically, there was enough oil in the can to have burned five hours. Surely we can do better than this, no?* ■

■ **ABOVE:** *I found that a wide-mouth canning jar lid would (just barely) cover an empty tuna can. It does not nest comfortably in place but neither does it fall   into the can.* ■

■ **ABOVE:** *A canning-jar ring holds the canning-jar lid securely in place. The original contents of the can have been replaced with clear cooking oil. I punched a hole in the center to hold the wick plus four smaller holes for drainage. Excess oil simply drains back into the font. ("Font" or "fount" is the proper term for the part of a lamp that holds the fuel.)* ■

■ **ABOVE:** *There's no law that says a tuna fish can must be used as the font. Here I've taken the same lid and installed it on a canning jar. And there's no law that says it must be a wide-mouth canning jar. A regular jar would work just as well.* ■

■ **ABOVE:** *And there's no law that says we must detach the lid. Here's a pork-and-beans can with the lid ¾ removed. We can bend up the cut portion to remove the beans as well as add oil. I punched the wick hole and the drain holes into the lid before using the can opener (so as to leave the lid with sufficient strength to resist the punching). It works well. Pork and beans, tomato soup, sweetened condensed milk. Is nothing sacred?* ■

Design #5 – Floating (Cork)

One problem with the beer-bottle lamp (and the tuna-can lamp as well) is that, once the fuel is consumed to a critical height, the wick's capillary action is insufficient to lift oil to the flame. One solution is a floating wick that rides up and down with the oil level and maintains the flame at a constant distance from the fuel.

My best design (i.e. one I dreamed up myself) is made from a 5-inch length of wire and small disks of cork (½" in diameter and ¼" thick). Admittedly, finding natural cork can be a problem in this day and age. Wine bottles are a possible source but beware of artificial corks. They are very dense and heavy. Natural cork has great buoyancy and, although it will get coated with oil and be greasy to handle, it won't soak up the vegetable oil and sink.

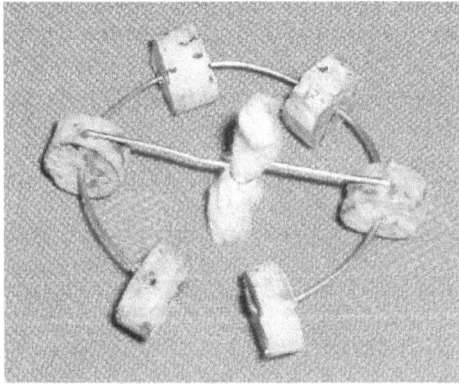

■ **ABOVE:** *The float assembly is shown upside down to illustrate its construction. In use, if the cross-wire holding the wick is on top (between the surface of the oil and the flame), it tends to choke off the fuel supply. Although counter-intuitive, it works much better if the assembly is flipped over and the wick-holding wire is underwater. Make that under-oil.* ■

People get strange ideas. The first vegetable oil lamp I ever saw was at a ritzy party. At every table, water dyed with food coloring had been poured in the bottom of a small glass bowl. A layer of vegetable oil floated on top of the water. A flame floated on top of the oil. Light from the flames shone through the oil and the colored water and onto the white tablecloths – an elegant effect in a darkened room.

Years later, working on this chapter, I showed this floating wick design to a lady I'd known since childhood. She looked puzzled. "You forgot the water. Don't you need water in the bottom of the bowl?" It stopped me cold.

"No. Water doesn't burn. Colored water is for looks only."

She didn't quite dare challenge me but serious doubt was written all over her face.

Design #6 – Floating (Ancient Pattern)

■ **ABOVE:** *A floating-wick design I adapted from a truly ancient pattern. It's a triangle of aluminum (from a beer can) with a paper-punch hole in the center for the wick. A sewing needle*

holds the wick in place. Cork is super-glued to the corners of the triangle. ∎

Design #7 – Floating (Kearny)

∎ **ABOVE:** *The same folks at Oak Ridge National Labs that gave you the Kearny Fallout Meter (KFM) to monitor radiation also came up with the floating-wick vegetable oil lamp shown here (intended for use in your fallout shelter). Their design looks to be a carved, one-piece model whereas mine, as you can see below, is tacked together from scrap lumber. ∎*

■ **ABOVE:** *The board under the flame doesn't catch fire because there is a layer of oil between the flame and the wood. The biggest disadvantage I see in this design is that the high ends of the wooden float obstruct (some) light from escaping the lamp and getting out into the room.* ■

Bad Info – Water Candle (DANGEROUS)

While on the floating theme, there's a danger that begs discussion.

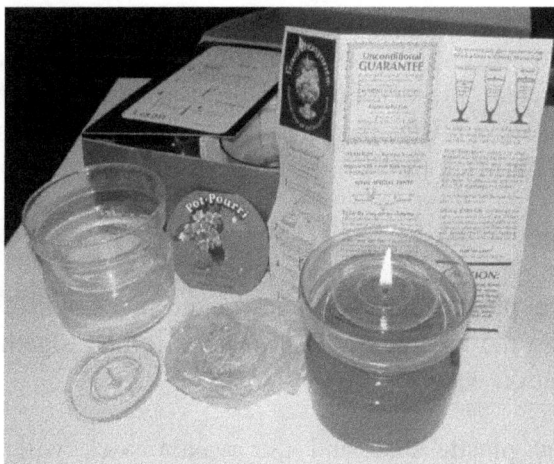

■ **ABOVE:** *Some years ago I chanced upon a carton of six commercially-made floating-wick olive oil lamps. The brand names on the box and/or paperwork were Anchor Hocking and Flam'buoyants. The directions contain this warning:* ***"CAUTION: Do not use benzene, kerosene, lighter fluid, perfumed, tinted 'lamp' or 'candle' oils."*** ■

Do not use kerosene? Thereby hangs a tale.

It involves a YouTube video by Taras Kulakov (a.k.a. The Mad Russian Hacker) for a "water candle." My apologies to Kulakov fans, but what the video presents is not safe.

It's not safe because of the recommended fuel: kerosene. And it's of concern here, in this olive-oil-lamp book, because the design strongly resembles an open-faced, vegetable-oil design.

So please bear with me while I discuss the water candle – how it works and where it fails.

The design is simple. First put some water in a glass, then add some kerosene. The kerosene floats on top of the water (just like olive oil would do). Next, add a wick.

The wick assembly for the kerosene water-candle is (1) a wick that's been removed from a birthday candle plus (2) a disc of clear plastic. For myself, I used a flat piece of plastic from a blister-pak. I poked a hole in the plastic and inserted the wick in the hole.

Here's how it works.

Both the plastic disc and the waxed wick will float on water. So the assembly, the two parts joined together, will also float on water.

Both the plastic disc and the waxed wick will sink in kerosene. So the assembly sinks in kerosene.

The bottom layer of the water candle is water. Above that, a layer of kerosene floats on top of the water. We add the wick assembly. It sinks in the kerosene but stops sinking when it reaches the water. The candle wick protrudes up out of the kerosene into the air where it can be lit with a match.

The wick, incidentally, coming as it does from a candle, has been impregnated with wax. That means the bottom of the wick that sticks down into the water won't soak up any water. If it did the lamp would sputter.

Now here's what's wrong with it.

I once measured a whole bunch of kerosene lamps –
antiques, brand new ones, boudoir lamps with small round
wicks, flat-wick lamps, wick-type lanterns, Duplexes,
Rayos, Aladdins – and every one was designed such that
the flame was a minimum of 1¾" away from the kerosene
in the tank. Most, in fact, were more than that. Rayo, for
example, was 2¾". These designs all came from Grandpa's
era. Back when people used kerosene every day of their
lives and understood the risks and knew what they were
doing.

Unfortunately, the YouTube "water candle" has zero space
between the flame and the kerosene. Zero.

Kerosene, like the gasoline in your car, is a petroleum
product, extracted from crude oil. Kerosene (depending on
grade) has a flash point between 100° F and 150° F (per the
Phillips 66 MSDS #682950 that you can view on-line:
http://www.coastoil.com/MSDS/Phillips%2066%20(Conoco)/Ke
rosene.pdf).

Vegetable oils are pressed from vegetables – corn, peanuts,
olives. They are thick, viscous, sticky. They all have flash
points above 400° F. They are all difficult to set on fire.
That's why this lamp would be safe with vegetable oil but
is dangerous with kerosene.

"Flash point" is defined as the lowest temperature at which
a liquid can form an ignitable mixture in air.

Okay, enough technical stuff. Here's the kerosene-powered
water candle in real time:

■ **ABOVE:** *The setup. The oil (red-dyed kerosene), plus water, wick, and plastic disc are in a Pyrex custard cup, setting on the concrete floor of my garage. Safety-wise, I'm a belt-and-suspenders kind of guy. So, to be extra safe in case the glass broke, I put the Pyrex cup inside an empty metal cookie box. Setting the arrangement on the floor provides a lot of headroom should the flames go high. The background is white to better photograph the black smoke.* ■

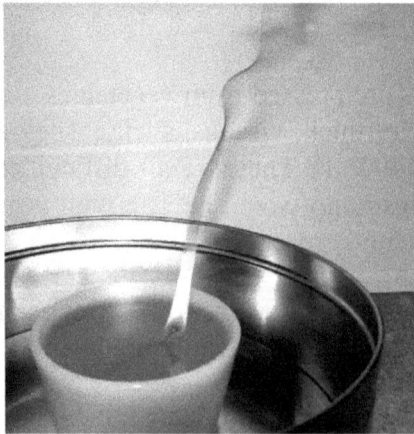

■ **ABOVE:** *And the smoke was plentiful. This is not a lamp you'd want inside your home. It would be like bringing inside a smudge pot from a construction site. Or removing the glass chimney from your kerosene lamp and turning the flame up.* ■

■ **ABOVE:** *Here we are at the one-hour mark. A runaway lamp. The YouTube video promoting this lamp has been viewed over 800,000 times and viewers' comments are all positive: "Cool man." "that's epic!!!!" "Nice idea." "Awesome." "Love it." Etcetera. My own comment is, "Wouldn't this would be great in the middle of your kitchen during a blackout?"* ■

I don't know which scares me more, the lamp's design or the viewers' reaction to it. Please note that what I've done here (think scientific method) is a repeatable experiment. You don't have to take my word for anything. You can perform the experiment yourself and draw your own conclusions.

Design #8 – String Lamps

There's a YouTube video showing an antique Japanese shokudai lamp (pronounced show-coo-dye). The lamp is shown and described but not demonstrated:
http://www.youtube.com/watch?v=A_o1TOvw6LI

The YouTube shokudai was made from terracotta (reddish, unglazed flower-pot material). It's one piece, but in principle was like a bowl and saucer glued together. Oil was in the bowl; a wick set in a small notch on the lip of the bowl and draped over the side. The flame burned just outside the notch. One side effect of this arrangement is oil being siphoned over the edge of the bowl by the wick and dripping onto the saucer. But at the nuisance of dripping, why can't we just use a bowl and saucer for a lamp?

We can except for one hitch. The bowl might break.

I tried using a small glass jar without a notch. But the wick, a heavy mop strand, kept slipping back over the edge and drowning the flame in the oil.

■ **ABOVE:** *So I made a notch with a bench grinder, touching the lip of the glass to the corner of the grinding wheel.* ■

It worked fine. The wick did not slip backwards into the oil. The flame did not jump over the edge of the glass and travel down the wick to the oil; the jar itself acted as a heat sink to prevent that.

I expected the glass to break. Ordinary glass, I thought, would not be able to take the unequal heat. But for the length of one evening at least, it did not break. So maybe I'm a Nervous Nellie. Or not.

The Japanese shokudai is kissin' cousin to the "string lamp" which uses, as the name implies, a simple string for a wick. The small diameter wick isn't heavy enough to drag the flame backwards and drown it in the oil so there's no need for a notch.

String lamp advantages: Fast, cheap, simple. Easy to light. Easy to adjust the size of the flame while burning. And, while each individual flame is small, you can use multiple wicks.

Disadvantages: It drips; a saucer under it is a must-have. You really should use a Pyrex dish or a metal tuna fish can. If you use regular glass, don't be surprised when it breaks. At least set the lamp in a pan big enough to catch everything. (With vegetable oil, breakage does not result in a major fire hazard but it sure creates one heck of a mess.)

I bought half a dozen mismatched Pyrex bowls (small custard dishes) at the Salvation Army store for 50¢ each. The markings and/or brand names on the bottom of the bowls were (1) Pyrex, (2) Glasbake, (3) Durable – Heat Resistant, and (4) Fire-King. I believe they're all borosilicate glass. Meaning they won't break if used as string lamps.

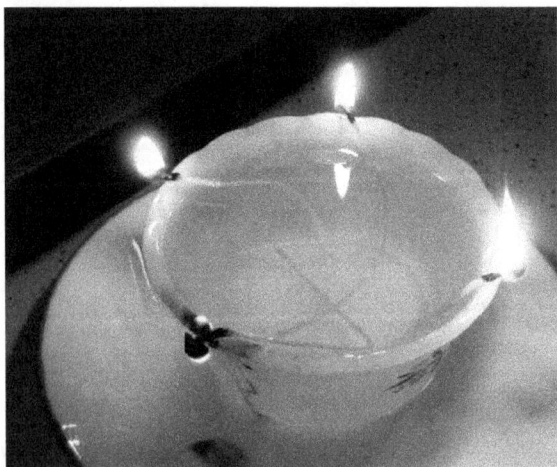

■ **ABOVE:** *This is a Fire-King brand bowl. Here a cinder has formed on one of the wicks. If you knock it off, the flame will resume undeterred. With four wicks, this lamp gives off a surprising amount of light.* ■

■ **ABOVE:** *A variation. It looks pretty but . . .* ■

■ **ABOVE:** *. . . where's the Pyrex when you need it?* ■

Fiberglass Wicks

Fiberglass wicks don't really work in string lamps. Fiberglass wicks are springy and don't drape limply over the edge of the bowl. After ten minutes, everything gets hot and slippery and the wick slides v-e-r-y s-l-o-w-l-y backwards into the soup. I'd recommend you stay with plain old droopy cotton string. Ya can't beat it.

Design #9 – Orange Peel

This one is more a dinner-party novelty than a utilitarian lamp. Clear glass (instead of orange peel) would allow more light to escape into the room. It does work, however, no denying that, and it gives a warm luminescence to the water in which it floats. If stylish sophistication during a blackout is your goal, then this is the lamp for you.

It's Hax's fourth design (although I've seen it in several other places). Half an orange peel serves as the font. The interior stem, left intact, serves as the wick. Because both the peeling and the stem have a high moisture content, I expected it to sputter. It didn't. It is terribly difficult to light, however. It took several tries, even when encouraged with a few drops of charcoal lighter fluid.

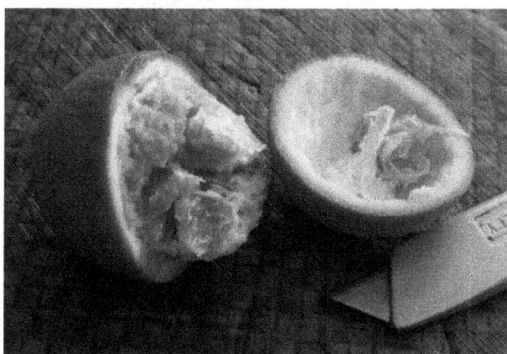

■ **ABOVE:** *The orange is scored all the way around and half the rind is gently peeled away in one piece. The interior stem is still attached. This was a navel orange. Other varieties might not be so cooperative.* ■

Bad Info – Veggie Oil in Kero Lamps

There's used to be a video (now disappeared) on YouTube from 'Dale Y the Green Guy' demonstrating olive oil in regular wick-type kerosene lamps. The video was followed by 17 comments saying it didn't work.

With the beer bottle lamp (Design #3), I found that the maximum vertical lift capability of a cotton wick in *vegetable oil* ranged from 1¾ to 2½ inches. It varied slightly with different oils.

But (as mentioned earlier) I've also measured a variety of *kerosene* lamps and the minimum distance between the flame and the fuel in the tank, even when the lamp is full, ranges from 1¾ to 2¾ inches.

Point is, the maximum distance that vegetable oil can be lifted is about the same as the minimum required.

I suspect the video maker deceived himself. I think he emptied a kerosene lamp and filled it with olive oil. But the wick was still saturated with kerosene. And he lit the kerosene and watched it burn and thought he was watching olive oil burn. At some point, the kerosene in the wick would be exhausted and only olive oil would remain. And a cotton wick will not lift olive oil that far.

Fat lamps

Moving along, lamps that burn semisolid animal fat are called fat-lamps. Variations are known as Betty lamps, Dutch lamps, stone lamps, grease lamps, slot lamps, and crusies. They will burn semisolid lard, butter, margarine, and Crisco (in addition to vegetable oil). The term crusie is Scottish; a "cruse" is a vessel for oil. The term Betty lamp comes from the German word "besser" or "bete," meaning *better*.

Design #10 – Tuna Can Fat Lamp

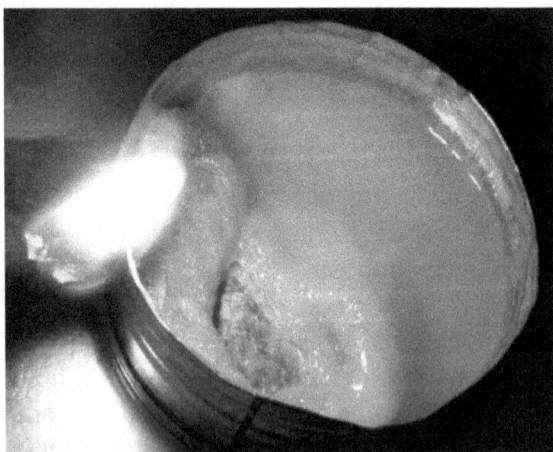

■ **ABOVE:** *This is likely the world's simplest fat lamp — the bottom portion of a tin can with a slot cut in the side to hold the wick. Remember, in tin can craft, all raw metal edges must be folded over and pinched together. Else you will cut yourself.* ■

Advantages: It's fast, cheap, easy to make. It can use multiple wicks. You can adjust the flame during the burn without interrupting the flame. And, like all the fat lamps shown here, it can burn vegetable oil as well as animal fat.

Disadvantages: It doesn't keep the fat melted very well. As shown in the first picture, the lard near the flame remained melted and was consumed right to the bottom of the can. On the other side of the can, however, the lard wasn't melted at all. That means maintenance is required during the burn to keep the fat pushed close to the flame.

Design #11 – Tuna Can Fat Lamp Variation

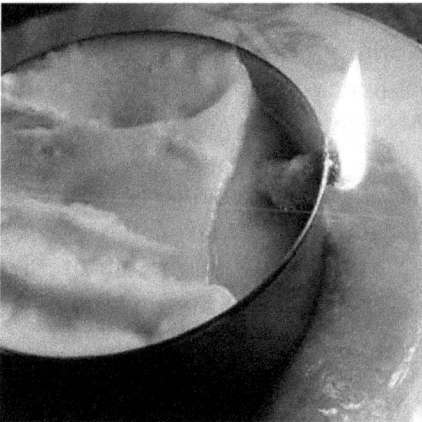

The wick is a strand from a cotton string-mop. And it must be cotton; synthetics melt. The fuel shown here is Crisco. Only the Crisco near the flame stays liquid. Every hour or so you must push a little fuel towards the flame. The tuna can sets on a saucer to catch drips. This is not the greatest lamp in the world but it works. Rudimentary lamps of this sort were what poor people lived with, day-in-and-day-out, before Edison's light bulb.

The wick needs to be prepped before you light it. "Prepping" means you saturate the wick in oil or grease before lighting. A dry wick poking out of a lump of Crisco won't get you very far.

Warning. This lamp is an open-faced lamp with an open flame. The flame is a mere whisker away from the fuel. It will safely burn heavy, viscous oils with a high flash point (olive oil) or semisolid fats (butter, lard). But it is not safe with most petroleum products (kerosene, for example, as we saw earlier with the "water candle").

Design #12 – Butter Candle

The butter candle is the final Hax design. I knew before I started that it wouldn't amount to much. The butter would quickly melt into a puddle. A string was too small to serve as a wick and give much light. The wick (with no core, no foot) would soon collapse and drown the flame in the liquid butter. Hey, I've been at this a while. I know how this stuff works. So the results surprised me.

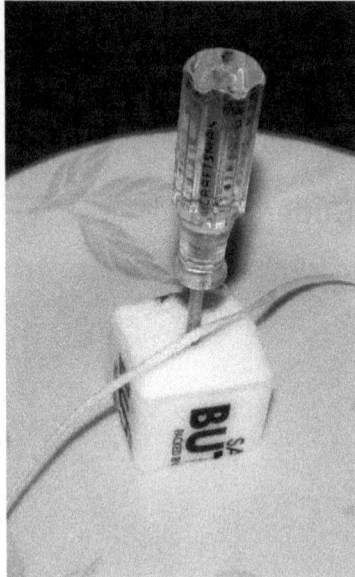

■ **ABOVE:** *A slice cut from a ¼-pound stick of butter, straight from the fridge. I left the paper wrapping in place to help with the melting-into-a-puddle problem. The piece shown here is not the end piece so there is no wrapping on the bottom. Hax uses a small Phillips screwdriver to punch a hole through the butter. A ⅛" drill bit or a nail would do the same. The wick is prepped with butter and pushed through the hole with the screwdriver.* ■

■ **ABOVE:** *Ten minutes into the burn the paper wrapping began to separate. So I wound a piece of Scotch tape around it on the fly (with the candle still burning). The patch worked well. After the first few minutes the flame was a respectable candle-size.* ■

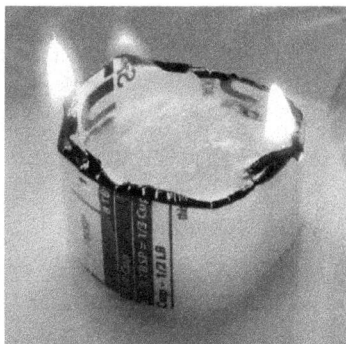

■ **ABOVE:** *At the one-hour mark, ⅛" of butter had been consumed. The butter was liquefied almost to the bottom. The wick collapsed (it can be seen on the right-hand side) but didn't drown the flame as I expected. Rather, it set fire to the paper rim. Ten minutes after this I had a saucer of melted butter for my popcorn. But, give the Devil his due, it did last for an hour, longer than I expected.* ■

Design #13 – Philippine Design

This design comes from the Philippines.

(1) Fill an empty and DRY baby food jar ⅔ full of sand. DRY sand. Common table salt also works. The purpose of the sand/salt is to hold the wick upright. Moisture in the sand will get into the wick and cause the flame to sputter.

(2) Pour vegetable oil into the jar. Stir it around so the sand on the bottom is saturated. You can see it through the glass. Then cover the sand with ¼-inch of oil. Don't fill the jar to the brim. Leave some space. There's a reason for this.

(3) The wick. Wrap some fluff from a cotton ball around a wooden toothpick or matchstick (remove the match head first). Personally, I start winding some cotton around one end of the stick as if making a Q-tip. Then I just continue winding for the entire length of the stick.

(4) In the center of the jar, insert the stick-wick into the sand. Push it right to the bottom. Height-wise, the top of the wick should be flush with the lip of the jar. It should not stick up out of the jar. Snip the wick shorter if necessary.

(5) Let the wick soak up some oil and light it. Use a drop of flammable liquid to help.

(6) Initially, it will probably burn too high and smoke. Instead of trying to cut or trim the wick down, do it the other way. Bring the oil level up. That's why you didn't fill the jar to the max to begin with.

This lamp will burn semisolid fat as well as vegetable oil.

To set up the lamp and initiate the burn, the semisolid fuel must be melted. Then, the same as when burning vegetable oil, fuel must be added to the lamp during the burn. In use, the fuel is consumed and more wick gradually exposed.

That means the flame gets bigger and begins to smoke. Because you can't trim the wick on this lamp while it is burning, you must add more fuel. And, with semisolid fuels, it must be melted before it can be poured in.

With vegetable oil, some fluff from a cotton puff wrapped around a toothpick suffices as a wick. But a heavier wick is needed for lard. I've found that *half* of a cotton mop strand works well. Each mop strand has four plies. I use two of the four, wrapped around a toothpick.

Advantages. Cheap, easy to make, simple materials. The flame, inside the jar, is somewhat shielded from breezes. The lamp is glass so light shines through its sides.

Disadvantages. Some maintenance is required during the burn; oil must be added as fuel is consumed and more wick is exposed (and the flame gets bigger). Adjusting the wick disturbs the flame. So don't adjust the wick. Adjust the oil level. Semisolid fuels (lard, butter) need to be melted before they are added.

Design #14 – I-Didn't-Know-Olive-Oil-Burned

The same folks who put out the *I Didn't Know That Olive Oil Would Burn* booklet also make a lamp that they sell through Lehman's. The lamp is intended to burn vegetable oil. I was delighted to discover that it burned lard as well.

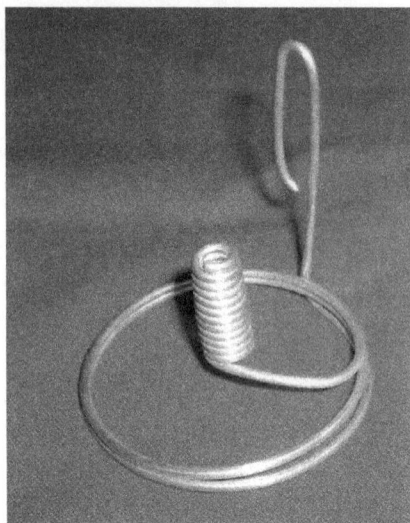

■ **ABOVE:** *The wick tube is a coil of wire. The same wire circles the bottom of the jar and keeps the wick tube centered.* ■

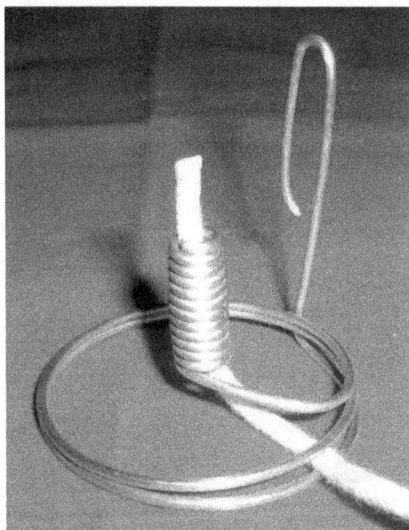

The wick, as you can see in the photos, is the same ordinary round wicking used in small kerosene lamps. I think kerosene wicking works successfully in this lamp because the metal wire leads heat from the flame right down into the fat. The result is hot, thin fuel that volatilizes well enough to support a flame even with close-knit conventional kerosene wicking.

Learning how to light this lamp is another matter. If, as I did, you pull the whole wire assembly out of the lamp and light it, you will singe some hair on the back of your knuckles attempting to re-insert it in the lamp. There is not enough clearance for the dangling wick and the wire circle to go through the mouth of the jar at the same time.

The answer is to not pull the wire assembly totally out of the jar. Instead, lift it by the little handle until the wire ring is near the top, then tilt the lamp, light the wick, and lower the wire back into the jar. Just like they tell you. When all else fails, read the directions.

On both the initial burn and subsequent replenishment, lard or butter must be pre-melted to pour into the lamp. On the other hand, if lard has merely hardened in the lamp from a previous burn, it will readily start with a drop of charcoal lighter fluid.

Advantages: The flame is inside the jar, somewhat shielded from breezes. On vegetable oil this lamp lights easily without starter fluid (unlike other designs). You can buy this lamp from Lehman's already made; you don't have to make anything.

Disadvantages: You must learn how to light it properly. It can only have one wick.

■ **ABOVE:** *The innards of the I-Didn't-Know-That-Olive-Oil-Would-Burn lamp operate just fine in a fancy dish.* ■

■ **ABOVE:** *A homemade knockoff works equally well. I wrapped my piece of wire around a nail.* ■

44

Design #15 – Copper End-Cap Fat Lamp

The copper fat-lamp is my own personal design. It burns both semisolid fuels as well as vegetable oil. Its secret lies in the use of copper. Copper transfers heat exceptionally well. Copper keeps the lard melted.

■ **ABOVE:** *Inside view. The font is a 1½" nominal-diameter copper end cap, found in the plumbing department of your hardware store.* ■

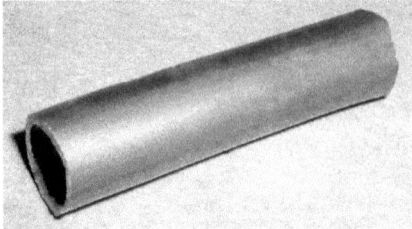

■ **ABOVE:** *The wick shelf or flame shelf is made from a piece of ¼ " copper tubing, 1½" long.* ■

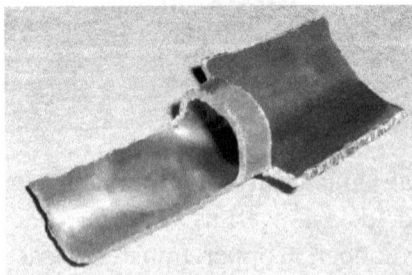

■ **ABOVE:** *Here's the tubing after being butchered with a hacksaw. One end will be the flame shelf. The other end will*

attach the shelf to the font. In the middle is a ring of tubing left intact that will encircle the wick and prevent it from sliding backwards into the font. It's also a heat sink so the flame does not follow the wick to the fuel source. ∎

∎ **ABOVE:** *The parts . . .* ∎

∎ **ABOVE:** *Assembled. The flame shelf is slanted. Drippings flow backwards into the font.* ∎

■ **ABOVE:** *A trivet-cum-carrier-cum-drip tray made from a small tin can. (I think pineapple juice came in this one.) The copper gets very hot. This accessory lets you carry it.* ■

■ **ABOVE:** *The carrier, another view.* ■

■ **ABOVE:** *Showing two wicks plus a lantern globe serving as a wind guard. And the lid from a metal can serving as the drip tray. Always remember the drip tray.* ■

A Word About Fuels

Something that does not work well in any lamp is bacon grease. Bacon slabs have brine – saltwater – injected into them for curing. The bacon grease retains some of the water. The water gets sucked into the wick and the lamp sputters as a result. Bacon grease will burn in a fat-lamp, but poorly.

Someone questioned me about using whale blubber such as the Eskimos use (or such as we imagine them using). I'm sure that it is *rendered* whale blubber, the same as lard is rendered pork fat. My mother used to stink up the house for days rendering pork fat from home-butchered hogs. Admittedly, the lard produced outstanding piecrust and homemade bread. But you have no idea how bad the rendering process smelled.

In whale blubber stoves, the heat from the stove is used for two purposes: (1) to cook supper and (2) to render additional oil so as to continue fueling the stove. The rendering process consists of gently cooking out the liquid fat or whale oil from the blubber. The oil thus obtained is then burned in the stove to render yet more oil, a self-sustaining process.

But this brings up the topic of fuels. With the exceptions of Design #3 and Design #4, above, all the lamps in this book are open-faced lamps. There is no physical barrier between the flame and the fuel and virtually no air gap. So what fuels are safe to run in such a lamp? Now there's a can of worms worth opening.

Let's do it . . .

In the case of cooking oil, smoke point refers to the temperature at which an oil begins to smoke. Above smoke point is flash point; above that is autoignition point, and above that is the flame temperature when the oil is burning. If the fuel in the well of an open-faced lamp is below its smoke point, then it is clearly safe to use.

For example, lard burns with a flame temperature of 1500° F. If you put lard in the copper fat-lamp (Design #15), after an hour the temperature of the melted lard reaches 130° F (where it remains). But the flash point of lard is 475° and the smoke point is 415°. A 130° fuel temperature versus a 415° smoke point looks pretty safe to me.

But mightn't the 1500° flame set off the melted lard? No. The oil would have to be at its flash point (475°) for that to happen and it's only 130°. In fact, that's how you'd extinguish the flame – by pouring a spoonful of melted lard over the top of it.

Corn oil likewise has an in-font temperature of 130° versus a smoke point of 400°. It, too, is safe. As is mineral oil (a petroleum product) with a smoke point of 280°. (Mineral oil, incidentally, is what lamp collectors substitute for whale oil in antique whale-oil lamps.)

As it turns out, SAFE fuels in open-faced lamps include animal fats, vegetable oils, and hydrogenated vegetable oils (e.g. Crisco, margarine).

NOTE: Not all "safe" fuels will work in all lamps. Some potential fuels such as lard, for example, are semisolid and must be kept melted. Some lamp designs will do it, some won't. Nor does "safe" mean a fuel necessarily smells good while burning.

NOT SAFE in open-faced lamps are alcohols: denatured alcohol, methanol (dry gas, Heet), ethanol, or isopropyl alcohol. Their temperature in the font (130° F) will be higher than their flash point(s) of around 50° F.

So far we've discussed vegetable oil, animal fat, and alcohol. Petroleum products are next and are a mixed bag.

A few specific petroleum products are safe in open-faced lamps. Vaseline is one example. Mineral oil (used as baby oil, laxative, and hydraulic fluid) is another.

But most petroleum products are not safe. Gasoline, white gas (Coleman fuel, Zippo lighter fluid), mineral spirits (paint thinner, charcoal lighter fluid), kerosene, jet fuel, diesel fuel, and home heating oil – none of these are safe in open-faced vegetable-oil lamps or fat lamps.

Why? Because the lamp's own flame will preheat the fuel and then ignite it. Go back and look at the "water candle" described earlier.

NOTE: The term smoke point has, with kerosene, an entirely different meaning from smoke point with cooking oil. With kero, smoke point is the maximum flame height, in millimeters, at which the fuel will burn without smoking.

Although smoke point is important in wick-fed lamps because it determines the degree of illumination possible from a given grade of kerosene, I've never seen it specified in an MSDS sheet.

Closing Notes

When burning, vegetable oil lamps and fat lamps have very little odor. (Little is not the same as none.) Surprisingly, it's kerosene lamps that need a chimney to stop the smoke and the smell.

Extinguishing a vegetable oil or fat lamp is another matter. If you merely blow it out, it will glow and smoke and stink. The solution is to pour a teaspoon of oil over the flame. With its oxygen cut off, it will be extinguished instantly with no smell and no smoke.

Don't forget your tweezers, an eyedropper, some charcoal lighter fluid, a sharp pick made from a nail or a wire coat hanger, and a rag to wipe your hands. They're all part of the kit necessary to make these lamps work.

These lamps are simple things but it would be good if you tried to make one of each kind before you need it. Knowing what works (for you) and what doesn't is invaluable. Like sex, reading about it and doing it are two different things.

Afterword

So far, on the lighting theme, I've published:

Lanterns, Lamps & Candles: A User's Guide – a CD in PDF format available from http://www.rc-publishing.com/. *Lanterns* is comprehensive: 70,000 words, 442 pictures.

The Amazing 2000-Hour Flashlight – available both as a Kindle ebook and in paperback from Amazon.

Book 1: Candles (from The Non-Electric Lighting Series) – both a Kindle ebook and in paperback from Amazon.

Book 2: Olive Oil Lamps &c. (from The Non-Electric Lighting Series) – as both a Kindle ebook and paperback.

I plan on publishing a sequence of 8-10 lighting books over the coming months as part of The Non-Electric Lighting Series. Coming soon to an Amazon near you . . .

www.ingramcontent.com/pod-product-compliance
Lightning Source LLC
Chambersburg PA
CBHW061754040426
42447CB00011B/2297